BRAZILIAN
JIU JITSU
TECHNIQUES

Also by Fabio Gurgel

BRAZILIAN JIU-JITSU / Advanced Techniques

BRAZILIAN JIU-JITSU
BASIC TECHNIQUES

Fabio Duca Gurgel do Amaral
Eight-time World Champion

BLUE SNAKE BOOKS
BERKELEY, CALIFORNIA

Dekel Publishing House

Dekel Publishing House
P.O. Box 45094; Tel Aviv 61450, Israel
www.dekelpublishing.com
ISBN 978-965-7178-11-9

Original Brazilian edition by **Axcel Books**
Published in North America by **Blue Snake Books/Frog, Ltd.**

Blue Snake Books/Frog, Ltd. books are distributed by North Atlantic Books
P.O. Box 12327, Berkeley, California 94712, USA

Chief Editor: Ricardo Reinprecht	**Production Editor:** Gisella Narcisi
Co-Editor: Alexandre Esteves	**Original Cover & Design:** Ingo Bertelli
Photography: Alexandre Vidal	**Photography Editor:** Carlos Alberto Sá Ferreira
Back Cover Photography: André Schiliró	**Opponent in photos:** Leonardo Vieira
English Translation: Pedro Rocha de Oliveira	**English Language Editor:** Efrat Ashkenazi
Book and Cover Design: Eldad Zakovitz	**Technical Advisor:** Branimir Tudjan

Printed in Israel

PLEASE NOTE: The creators and publishers of this book disclaim any liabilities for loss in connection with following any of the practices, exercises, and advice contained herein. To reduce the chance of injury or any other harm, the reader should consult a professional before undertaking this or any other martial arts, movement, meditative arts, health, or exercise program. The instructions and advice printed in this book are not in any way intended as a substitute for medical, mental, or emotional counseling with a licensed physician or healthcare provider.

Library of Congress Cataloging-in-Publication Data

Gurgel, Fabio Duca do Amaral
  Brazilian jiu-jitsu basics techniques : the jiu-jitsu handbook / Fabio Duca do Amaral Gurgel.
    p. cm.
  Orginally published by Axcel Books in Brazil."
  ISBN-13: 978-1-58394-165-2 (trade paper)
  ISBN-10: 1-58394-165-7 (trade paper)
  1. Jiu-jitsu--Brazil. I. Title.
GV1114.A93 2007
796.81--dc22
                        2006103301

1 2 3 4 5 6 7 8 9 Dekel Productions, Tel Aviv 12 11 10 09 08 07

Table of Contents

1

BASICS

This is where it all begins. The basic techniques are very important for the students' initiation, for they make them familiar with the tatami, the kimono, and the first moves. Rolls are directly responsible for the safety of the students, enabling them to fall without hurting themselves; the hip escape and the technical stand-up consist of educational movements which are very often used in combat. Properly learning these movements is vital for the development of future techniques. These basic techniques must never be neglected.

• FORWARD ROLL

Put yourself in position with one leg forward and the opposite hand on the floor, aligned with your foot. The hand on the same side as the lead leg must be placed with the fingers pointing backwards, and the head should be turned so as to look over the shoulder opposite the lead leg.

Put all your weight on the tip of the lead foot. Raise the rear leg from the floor, leaning forward into the fall.

Start to roll over your shoulder, gently but steadily, thus protecting your head from any contact with the ground.

During the roll, keep your legs extended and separated, and keep your hands over your chest.

At the end of the movement, your arm should fall completely extended, at a distance of one hand from your leg, which should also be extended and held parallel to the arm. Keep your chin pressed against your chest, and the other hand close to the belt.

• BACKWARD ROLL

Stand up.

1

2 Crouch by sitting on your heels and stretching your arms in front of you.

Sit down on the ground, pressing your chin against your chest and leaning back into the fall.

3

Slap both your arms on the ground, keeping your hips on the ground and both legs up and extended, completing the movement that protects your body in case you fall backward.

• FORWARD FALL

Stand up.

Bend your body forward, leaning over.

Throw back your legs, at the same time slapping the ground with both forearms and both hands while holding your stomach in, so as to keep your body off the ground. Your knees should not touch the ground at any time.

• TECHNICAL STANDUP

Start the position by lying down with the soles of your feet facing front.

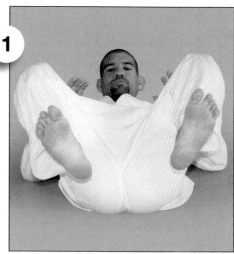

Sit up in defensive position with one leg extended and the other bent, one arm resting on the knee, and the other hand on the floor behind your right hip.

3 Propel yourself up with the foot which is on the floor, pulling your extended leg between the arm and the other leg, lifting both feet from the ground and supporting yourself only by means of one arm.

4 Touch the ground with the lead foot, aligning it with your hand, and throw the other leg back.

5 Stand up in ready stance, at a safe distance from your opponent.

• HIP ESCAPE

Start with both feet on the ground
and your legs bent.

Raise your hip,
supporting
yourself on two
feet and one
shoulder.

Put your foot on the floor opposite the side on which you turned, and extend
the other leg.

Slide your hip backwards, so that the foot of your extended leg touches your hand; extend your body and start over on the other side.

SELF-DEFENSE

Perhaps the most important part of Jiu-Jitsu, the basis of everything–despite its being overlooked by many–is self-defense. Only when the student has learned to defend himself can he begin the process of becoming a complete fighter capable of going up against practitioners of any other art. Do not delude yourself into believing that learning your guard well will save you from a real fighting situation: self-defense must be learned and trained as much as, or more than, the competitive part of Jiu-Jitsu. It will be the source of all your self-confidence and will give you the bearing of a great fighter.

• TWO-HANDED FRONT CHOKE

The attacker grasps your neck with both hands in an attempt to choke you.

Defense begins by placing your chin over your chest in order to prevent the attacker from pressing his thumbs on the windpipe area. You must simultaneously hold the stance and keep your balance, with both legs slightly bent so as to form a stable base.

Turn your head, releasing it from one of the attacker's arms, thus removing the pressure exerted by his hands.

The movement ends with a step backwards, assuming combat position.

• COLLAR GRAB

In this situation, the attacker grabs the collar of your jacket or shirt.

It is important that you place your hand correctly, observing the position of the aggressor's hand (in our example, his thumb is turned up). Use both hands in your defense: put one hand around the attacker's wrist, in the form of a cup, and the second next to his elbow, with your thumb directly over the joint...

3 ...while taking a diagonal step forward in order to put your foot outside the opponent's feet and raising his elbow. It is important to hold your elbow against your chest so as to create a lever, which will keep the opponent from lowering his arm.

Turn your hips, bending your legs so as to allow you to move backwards, holding your opponent's arm high. **4**

5 Move behind your opponent, grabbing his wrist and moving the arm that had been on his elbow over to his neck. Pull his wrist up, so as to complete an armlock.

• STANDING REAR CHOKE

The aggressor grabs hold of your neck from behind.

1

2

Immediately grab his wrist and elbow, falling in ready stance with both legs bent and eyes facing the ground.

Extending your legs, lift your opponent off the ground.

3

4 Project your hip upwards, pulling the aggressor's arm towards you and twisting your torso so that your elbow is drawn diagonally towards your knee.

Hold your opponent's wrist to keep his arm extended. **5**

• CHOKE DOWN FROM BEHIND

The aggressor approaches from behind and prepares to attack.

After executing a choke hold from behind, the aggressor puts his leg between yours, in order to bend your body backward. First, grab hold of his arm, putting one hand on his wrist and the other as high as his elbow, keeping both your elbows close to your body in order to relieve the pressure of the choke.

3

Take one step back with the leg on the same side as his attacking arm.

4

Take advantage of the fact that your opponent is leaning his body weight back, and make a 180° turn toward his attacking arm; keep your supporting foot behind the aggressor's leg, and bend your body forward so as to make him lose his balance.

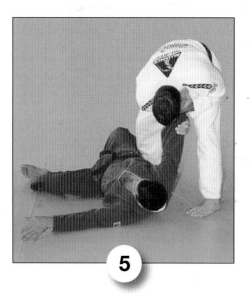

5

Keeping both feet in place, pull your opponent down, making him fall and pinning his arm at the end of the movement.

• BEAR HUG OVER THE ARMS FROM THE FRONT

The aggressor bear-hugs you over the arms. Your options are either to throw him down or lift him off the ground.

Immediately place both hands on his hips, and go into a stance with your hips thrust back. The lever thus created will make his attack impossible.

Take one step towards the side opposite the direction you are facing, hugging your opponent's back with one hand and keeping the other hand on his hips to maintain the necessary distance.

4 Move in front of your opponent, preparing a hip throw, and move your hand from his hip to his arm.

Execute the hip throw.

5

6 Complete the throw by pinning his arm.

• BEAR HUG OVER THE ARMS FROM THE REAR

The aggressor bear-hugs you from behind, pinning your arms.

First, free your arms by bending your legs slightly and falling into the ready stance.

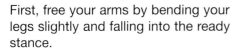

Put one foot behind your opponent, grabbing both his knees with your hands, on the outer side of his legs.

Lift your opponent off the ground.
To do this, you must keep your eyes
on your supporting foot—the foot
opposite the side on which you lifted
your opponent—in order to keep
your balance. Also, make sure you
do not keep holding your opponent
throughout the entire movement.
Let him down as soon as you begin
having difficulty in keeping your eyes
on your supporting foot.

When you release the attacker's legs during the
movement, take advantage of the time it takes him to
fall, in order to grab his arm and turn your body in the
direction opposite that of the movement. This will place
you in a dominant position, from which you can proceed
to execute an armlock or any other kind of attack.

• SHOULDER GRIP

The aggressor grabs hold of you by the shoulder, trying to either push you back or pull you towards him.

Place yourself beside the aggressor and move your arm over and around the arm that is holding you. Make sure your movement is not too wide, so as not to give the aggressor a chance to withdraw his arm.

After executing your movement, place your elbow close to your ribs and your forearm directly behind your aggressor's elbow joint. A good **3** clue for knowing whether your arm is correctly positioned is to check if the tip of the elbow is as high as the middle of your cuff.

Grab your own wrist with your other hand, the palms of your hands turned upwards. Drive your elbow upward **4** and forward, keeping yourself upright, and you will have your shoulder grip.

• BEAR HUG BELOW THE ARMS FROM THE REAR

The aggressor clasps you around the waist from behind, under your arms.

Defense begins by placing both hands on the floor in order to keep the aggressor from lifting you off the ground. After that, put one of your hands on his heel and, being in the ready stance, bend your legs.

Make sure your hip is directly over the opponent's knee, and then pull his foot up between your legs while pressing down with your hip, forcing your opponent off balance.

4 Hold up the opponent's heel with both hands, while pressing his knee with your hip, thus trapping him in a knee lock.

PASSING THE GUARD

This chapter, which discusses how to pass the guard, is somewhat more complex than the previous one. Like everything about Jiu-Jitsu, you rely on your opponent's reactions in order to properly apply the correct technique at a given moment. Thus, there is no preferred technique for passing the guard; there is just the better time for it to be used! Still, even when you choose the right time, you must rely on your opponent's defense. That is where the combinations come in, which are, in fact, the real secret about passing the guard.

Knowing how to use variations is a key factor for a successful pass. Therefore, it is essential that you train in each technique separately, and start practicing the variations between them only after you have mastered each one separately. You will then open a wide range of possibilities, developing your capacity to create indefensible situations. Another indispensable factor is rhythm: once you reach a good passing position, you must keep your opponent in permanent difficulty, blocking any attempt to attack or sweep. This too will depend on your variations, because if you have a new form of attack prior to each new defense attempted by your opponent, you will be sure to accomplish your goal.

• POSTURE

When in guard posture you must pay special attention to your hands, which must always be in palms-down position, and to your arms, which must always be extended: one arm placed further away from you, in order to press your opponent's torso against the ground, and the other next to you, so as to immobilize his hips, blocking any attempt to apply an armlock.

After achieving the correct posture, start to stand up. Always begin by raising the leg on the same side as the arm that is further from your body, so as to keep your balance.

The next step is to pick yourself up, making sure the elbow of the arm which is placed over the opponent's hips is turned towards you and always extended, and pressing down on the opponent's hips. Also, be sure to bend your legs slightly, placing them at shoulder width, in order to retain a good stance.

Open your legs. You can then start any kind of guard pass you prefer.

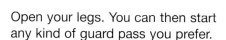

• POSTURE WITH HANDS ON ARMPITS

There are several ways to open a guard, but this is one of the best ways to obstruct an attack. You need to place one hand in each lapel and put the lapels well under your opponent's armpits, forcing his torso against the ground. While doing so, keep the palms of your hands facing down.

Rise up slightly in order to put some space between your hips and his. To do this, take one step back. Then put one of your knees between your opponent's legs, keeping the other behind you, and start to get up, forcing your opponent to open his legs.

With the guard already open, grab the hem of his trousers with the hand on the same side as the leg that is thrust further back. Bend your other arm slightly, so that your elbow remains over your opponent's hips.

Take one sidestep and at the same time, press down on your opponent's leg. Keep both legs extended so that your hips can be held high, and lower your head towards the opponent's belly. Note that you have to put some pressure on his hips, using your elbow.

Place your knee against his hip, at the same time leaning your body weight over him, while still grabbing his leg with your hand.

Remove your hand from his leg and dominate his neck.

• PASSING THE GUARD WITH HANDS INSIDE

After opening your opponent's legs, begin passing the guard by putting your hand which was on his chest between his legs. Keep the elbow of your other arm inside, always facing you.

Put your hand deep in your opponent's collar with your thumb on the inside, raising his leg over your shoulder. Put your knee on the ground so that you can bring your shoulder under your opponent's leg.

Thrust forward with all your weight, supporting yourself on the tips of your toes and drawing up your opponent's hips by the back of his trousers.

4

See, from a different angle, how you should grab the back of your opponent's trousers, in order to raise his hips. Also note the position of your legs and feet.

Lower your hips and raise your head so that your opponent's legs go around and past your face. Next, with your rear hand, push down on your opponent's trousers, placing his hips on the ground again.

5

6

Dominate your opponent, releasing his collar, putting your elbow beside his ear, and placing your other hand on the ground on the opposite side, next to his hips.

• PASSING THE GUARD PUSHING THE KNEES

Open your opponent's legs. Grab
them firmly, with your hands on
his trousers, on the inner side of
his knees, and take a small step
backwards.

Step aside, distancing yourself
from his legs. Remain standing and
holding his legs.

Propel your
shoulder over
your opponent's
belly, extending
your arms so
as to place his
legs on the
ground.

4 Lean with your weight on your opponent's shoulder, placing your knee against his hips, stretching your other leg, still keeping your hand in the same place.

Release your opponent's leg and embrace him, pressing your chest over his, and putting one arm behind his neck and the other under his arm.

5

• PASSING THE GUARD WITH KNEE INSIDE

After opening guard, move the hand that had been placed over your opponent's chest to his leg, forcing it down to the ground. Bend your other arm, supporting the elbow on your thigh.

1

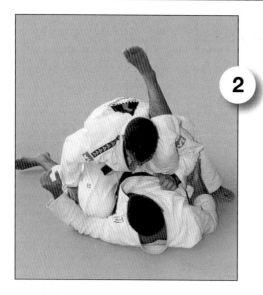

2

Put your knee forward, over the leg that was lowered, while moving the other hand around and inside your opponent's other leg.

Move the hand that went past the leg straight to the opponent's collar, grabbing it with the thumb turned inward. Lean your body weight forward.

3

4

Clasp the opponent's head with the hand that was on his leg.

5 Cross the other knee over the leg that is stretched on the ground, keeping both knees together and immobilizing the opponent's leg, with both your feet remaining on the other side of his leg.

Take both your feet off at the same time, placing your opponent in side control.

6

• PASSING THE GUARD CROSSING THE KNEES

In this variation, your hand is on the opponent's hips in order to force his leg down, holding it by the thigh and pressing it against the ground.

1

2 Cross your knee over the leg that was lowered, pressing your other elbow on your opponent's hips.

Grab hold of his arm by pulling it up, at the same time placing your other hand under the opponent's other arm. **3**

4 See, from a different angle, the position of your feet and arm under your opponent's arm.

Thrust the foot that was over the opponent's leg forward, so that it passes under your other leg, finishing the movement with your hips turned on the side and your opponent completely dominated.

• PASSING THE HALF-GUARD

Note how you should be positioned when beginning this pass. The foot that is pinned should be close to the hips, keeping the knee bent in a 90° angle. Lean heavily on your shoulder over your opponent, pressing his chin so as to force him to face outward. Your hand must be on his hips, serving as a support for your elbow to help you release your leg from his lock.

2 After you release your leg, pulling it up as high as your opponent's knee, place your knee on the ground. Keep pushing his knee with your hand, so that it cannot regain hold of your leg.

Put your hand beneath the opponent's arm with which he will try to push your knee, and crawl up with that hand open. **3**

4 Slide your other knee under your opponent's armpit, while forcing his arm up, so that only your foot remains pinned.

5

Place your hand on the opponent's collar with your thumb inward, pressing the elbow against the ground. This will force your opponent to turn onto his other side, thus releasing the foot he still held. You have got him on mount.

• PASSING THE GUARD WITH ONE HAND ON THE LEG AND THE OTHER INSIDE HIS COLLAR

Starting from the same position as in the previous pass, the opponent now defends his guard by drawing his leg back over your shoulder, blocking your movement.

Place your knee over his pinned leg, simultaneously moving your hand from his belt to his collar, grabbing it with your thumb on the inside.

3 Release his leg and hug his head, still holding his collar with your other hand, pinning his leg with your shin and leaning your body weight over his knee and over the elbow of the same side.

Lie sideways on one hip, keeping your knee over his leg and throwing back the other leg.

4

5 Turn your hip back again and dominate the guard.

SWEEPS

This chapter discusses sweeps. Undoubtedly, the sweep is the most evolving technique of Jiu-Jitsu competition nowadays, and also one of the most complex to learn and train. The principle of sweeps is one of balance: anyone who is only partially on the ground is already off balance. Each situation thus has its own particular sweep, together with the proper lever effect we should seek in order to accomplish a more precise movement. Like everything about Jiu-Jitsu, we will face an opponent who will try to do exactly the opposite of what we want, and that is why there are sweep combinations. For instance, if we try a sweep in which our opponent is to be projected forward, he will naturally try to put his weight to the rear in order to defend himself. It is precisely at this time that we bring in the combination, using a sweep that will throw him in whatever direction his weight can help us most. If we have a good sweep repertoire, every time our opponent is even slightly off balance we will have the chance to try different sweeps until one of them is successful. Training in these techniques is very important, for it is often the case that a slight imbalance will lead not only to a sweep, but to a finish as well.

• SCISSORS SWEEP

The opponent is in the right posture, but first he moves the leg opposite his lead arm forward.

Open the leg by placing your calf over your opponent's thigh, simultaneously escaping with your hips to the same side.

Move in with your shin, pressing it against your opponent's stomach, leaving only the foot on the outside. Turn your other leg over on the side, laying it down on the ground next to his supporting knee. Keep your hand on his collar during the entire movement.

4 Move the bent leg that is on your opponent's stomach as if you were kicking a ball, while moving the other leg in the opposite direction, in a scissors-like motion.

5

Taking advantage of your opponent's imbalance, roll over him to the mount position, keeping your hand on his collar during the entire movement.

• SCISSORS SWEEP WITH BACK HOOK

The starting position is the same as that of the scissors sweep. Place a hook behind your opponent's leg.

Prepare again to execute a throw, taking special note of how you should place your foot on his belt and also of how your knee must be kept inside your opponent's arm.

Attempting to avoid the throw, the opponent kneels down, which creates a new imbalance.

Extend your leg on the outside, in order to set your opponent's knee against it. Using your arms, make a rapid movement as if you were trying to cross your opponent's arms, and simultaneously force your knee inwards.

Dominating the opponent's arms, pull yourself up.

Finish in mount position.

• BELT SWEEP

Your opponent is in guard, but has not immobilized your upper body.

Move into a sitting position, placing your arm diagonally over the opponent's shoulder, holding his belt and stretching your other arm behind you against the ground.

Open your legs, raise your hips and turn your torso so as to face the ground. Note that the fingers of your supporting hand are facing forward, opposite your body.

Move the hand that was on your opponent's belt to his elbow, pressing it against your chest, so that he cannot use this arm to support himself.

Roll over and dominate your opponent, opening your arms and gaining balance.

• LEG SWEEP

Your opponent prepares his posture, but he uses the wrong leg again.

Put your hand inside the leg he has just raised, firmly holding his opposite elbow. Open your legs and slide your hips towards this side.

3 Press your leg under the opponent's armpit, pushing him back towards the side on which he has no support. At the same time, bend your other leg, so that it does not remain under your opponent's body at the end of the movement.

Prop yourself up on your elbow, drawing his leg towards you.

4

5 As the movement ends, you are on top of him, in a perfect mount.

• REEL SWEEP

The opponent is standing in good
posture.

Put both your hands on his heels,
closing your knees against his chest
and thrusting your hips forward, so
as to push him back.

After the opponent falls down, he will try to support himself in order to get up
again. Support yourself on your hand that is on the ground and move your other
hand diagonally in order to grasp his supporting arm.

Pull his arm up and thrust your hips forward, extending your leg.

4

Move the dominated arm to the other side, so that you can bend your stretched leg, knee down, and complete the mount.

5

• TUMBLE SWEEP

Grab both your opponent's arms from behind his elbows, using his sleeves.

1

2 Pull his elbows towards you, and place both your feet on his groin, bending your legs.

Then stretch your legs up, propelling your opponent over your head. **3**

Once you feel that his weight has fallen back, close your elbows to keep him from supporting his hands on the ground, and roll back over your shoulder.

4

5

Hold your opponent in mount.

• HALF-GUARD SWEEP

While under your opponent, clasp
his arm on the same side as his
dominated leg, grabbing his kimono
as high as his back in order to
prevent him from pushing your leg
and trying a mount. Draw up your
other arm, placing your knee against
his hip and using the outside leg to
pin down his leg.

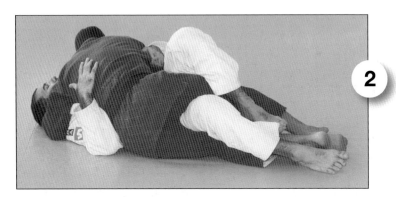

Remain in
the same
dominating
position,
establishing a
support with
your other leg
outside your
opponent's leg.

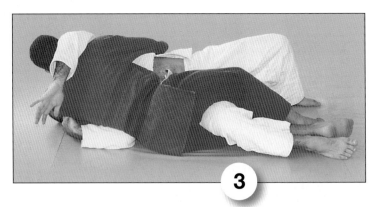

In a single movement, place your foot on the ground as a
support, and create a bridge by extending your arm, so as
to move your opponent's head with your biceps and make
him lose balance.

Turn your opponent over and dominate him in a half-guard. This technique, as well as all sweeps, is worth two points in a competition.

• FEET-ON-GROIN SWEEP WITH HOOK

Begin your work on the open guard, placing your foot on the opponent's groin and dominating his arm and leg on the same side. Make sure your hips are turned to the other side and your other foot is against his biceps.

Move your hand from the opponent's collar to his arm, and then grab his heel with the other hand, keeping your feet firmly in the same position.

Take advantage of the moment in which your opponent tries to extricate his arm, because he will fatally lean his weight back. This will give you the right timing to move your foot from his biceps to the back of his heel, forming a hook with your instep.

Now, simultaneously push the foot that is on his groin, pull the heel with your hand and raise your hook in the direction in which his foot is pointing, usually diagonally in front of him.

Complete the position by placing yourself over your opponent. You will most often be able to get him in a half-guard, but a mount is not impossible, and neither is a guard.

SIDE ATTACKS

The attacks for the side control position are highly diversified. This is also a position of extreme control. However, the fear of losing position often deters people from risking attack, and they limit themselves to pinning down their opponents, resulting in a game with only a few offensives. I believe in a bold Jiu-Jitsu, which seeks a finish in any position, especially in one so rich in attacks. You need only to keep some guidelines in mind: position your weight so as to keep your body relaxed at all times, for tension makes you more susceptible to inversion and obviously causes you to expend excessive energy. Almost all attacks in this position can be easily replaced by others. With a little practice, you can begin to create countless finishing situations originating from any move, which means that your opponent will find it very difficult to defend himself.

Remember: the attacks must be tight, leaving no space for escape, unless such space is created for your own benefit. Do as an efficient chess player would, and close off all defense options until it is time for checkmate.

• CHOKE

You have your opponent in side control. Place your elbow against his ear and your arm under his shoulder, in order to keep him firmly in place.

With the hand that was next to the opponent's hips, grab his collar with the palm of your hand turned up, stretching your leg outward, in order to create the necessary space for your hand to pass between your chest and your opponent's.

After grabbing hold of your opponent's collar, lean your elbow against his diaphragm, turning your hips slightly aside so as to make it easier for your other hand to come in and grasp his collar, this time with your thumb on the inside.

Lower your head and straighten your hips, tightening the choke. It is important not to open your elbows, but rather to draw your opponent towards your chest.

4

• SIDE CONTROL ARMLOCK

In side control, take advantage of the unfavorable position of your opponent's holding your back, and twist your arm around his, grasping his collar.

1

2

Move up to his head, keeping your arm wound as tight as possible.

3 Keeping one knee on each side of your opponent's head, shift the weight of your head to the opposite side of your wound-up arm, forcing him to turn aside.

Place your knee against the opponent's ribs on the same side as the twisted arm, slightly raising your head.

4

5 Place both feet on the ground and sit back, pulling the opponent's arm and finishing with an armlock.

• KIMURA

Begin the attack in side control, with one arm around your opponent's shoulder and the other beside his hips, to prevent him from regaining his guard.

Place your knee over his stomach, forcing him to try to displace it.

With the hand on the same side of the knee, grab your opponent's wrist and push it towards the ground, at the same time moving your other arm under his arm and grabbing your own wrist. Note that the grab is always done with all five fingers up.

Take your knee from his stomach, reverting to side control, but now change your stance, and keep his arm dominated as before.

Pass your leg over your opponent's head and raise his elbow on the same side. Supporting your own elbow on the ground, push his wrist towards your foot.

• SIDE CONTROL KIMURA

In side control, take advantage of the unfavorable position of your opponent's holding your back, and twist your arm around his, grasping his collar.

Move up to his head, keeping your arm wound as tight as possible.

After moving into this position, the opponent tries to withdraw his arm, passing it in front of your face. Grab his wrist with your free hand and press down on your own wrist with the hand that was on his collar.

4 Pull up the opponent's arm by raising your torso and keeping it pressed close to his arm.

Push his hand towards his back, always keeping the arm bent (the smaller the angle, the better the lever), and you have taken him in the Kimura.

5

• TURNAROUND ARMLOCK

You are in side control, with your arm under your opponent's head.

1

Put both hands on the ground, locking your head and placing your knee on his stomach. Make sure that the other leg is extended and that your foot is on the ground.

2

When your opponent tries to push your knee, grab his triceps with the palm of your hand facing up, leaning with your elbow on his ribs.

3

4

Take one sidestep with the other leg, pulling up the arm that you had attacked.

Turn around while sitting down, and complete the armlock.

• INVERTED ARMLOCK

You have your opponent in side control. He clasps your shoulder, placing his arm between your head and your arm.

Wrap your arm around him, grabbing your own collar and placing your other hand on the ground on the same side.

Stretch your supporting arm and place your knee on your opponent's stomach, raising your torso and placing your elbow joint over his.

Pass your leg over his head and sit back. Do not lie back, just keep sitting.

Move your other hand over your elbow and press down on it to complete the movement.

• KNEE-ON-STOMACH CHOKE

Starting from side control, put one of your hands on your opponent's collar, with the thumb on the inside, and with the other, grab his hip on the same side. Press your elbows downward.

With a small jump, place one knee on your opponent's stomach and extend your other leg. The foot of the leg that is over your opponent's stomach must not touch the ground, since your whole shin must be against your opponent's belly.

Bring the hand that was on his hips in under the other arm, with the palm of the hand facing up so as to grab the back part of your opponent's collar.

Remove your knee from his stomach and put it on the ground close to your opponent's hips, so as to maintain your balance. Lower your head and tighten your choke.

• KNEE-ON-STOMACH ARMLOCK

Starting with
your leg on
your opponent's
belly, begin to
prepare the
choke.

As your opponent attempts to defend
himself, grasp his crossed arm and
pull it up.

Pass the leg that was stretched over
the opponent's head and to the other
side, keeping his arm inside.

Sit back with your hips, as close as possible to your opponent's body, pulling his arm and firmly grabbing hold of his wrist, finishing in an armlock.

6

MOUNTED ATTACKS

We have now arrived at Jiu-Jitsu's supreme position, one of extreme superiority and total domination, but also very detailed, for imbalance is constant here and you must know how to use it to your own advantage. Imbalance will often bring you benefits, but you must train very hard if you want to find your own point of balance and comfort when mounted. Choking is an excellent starting point for attacks in this position, since it is sufficient for you to put one hand on your opponent's collar for him to start worrying about being choked, and it is precisely this worry that allows you to achieve a better position. It is very important not to remain sitting on your opponent's belly, once it has become his main point from which to create a lever for displacing your weight and making you lose balance. Therefore, you should put your knees forward in order to crouch on your heels; this can also give you the option of an arm attack, in addition to the choking.

• CLASSIC CHOKE

Starting from mounted position, open your knees to improve your balance and raise your torso to facilitate your attack.

With one hand, slightly lift your opponent's collar so that you can slide your other hand in as deeply as possible, with the palm facing upwards.

Put your other hand in place, also with the palm up, but make sure you move it under the first hand, so that your wrists are straight and firm.

4 Put your head on the ground, on the same side as the first hand (which is crossed over the other), creating the necessary support to tighten your choke once more, pulling the opponent towards your chest and keeping your elbow closed.

• THUMB CHOKE

In mounted position, with your first hand placed as in the classic choke, start to move your other hand in, leading with your thumb.

1

2 Place your thumb inside the opponent's collar. The other four fingers should remain outside his kimono.

3 Turn your wrist as much as possible, in order to make the necessary adjustment.

Place your forehead on the ground next to your other hand, exerting pressure so as to tighten the choke once again, drawing the opponent towards your chest.

4

• SLEEVE CHOKE

You are mounted and hugging your opponent's head; your body's weight should be on the supporting arm on the same side of your head. You must be able to rely on this supporting arm in case your opponent attempts an Upa.

1

2 Grab your own sleeve with the hand embracing your opponent, with all fingers except the thumb on the inside.

Place your closed hand over your opponent's neck. Your hand must get near his biceps.

3

4 Extend the arm that you had placed over your opponent's neck, forcing it towards the ground, and finish by pulling the sleeve and executing the choke.

• ARMLOCK

You are in mount position with your knees thrust forward, directly under your opponent's armpits, making it difficult for him to escape.

Your opponent starts trying to escape, putting his hands under your armpits. Place your hands on the ground to regain balance, and choose which arm to attack.

Move the leg opposite the chosen arm forward, so as to remain with two supports: your shin and your hand, which must be aligned with your opponent's head.

4

Lie back, slipping your foot under the opponent's head and grabbing his wrist with both hands to execute an armlock. You must slide your knee continuously until you finish the attack.

• CLASSICAL ARMLOCK

You are mounted. The opponent pushes you on the chest.

1

2 Place both hands over your opponent's chest, passing one of them over his outstretched arm.

Leaning your weight on the opponent's chest, move your leg towards the side opposite his outstretched arm, standing on your knee and turning your hips, so as to immobilize his elbow and prevent him from freeing his arm.

3

4 Keeping your hands on his chest, move your leg over his face, sitting on his shoulder.

Sit back, first clasping your opponent's arm and then grabbing hold of his wrist with his thumb turned up. Bend your legs and press your knees inward, and then raise your hips and complete the armlock.

• KEY LOCK

You are mounted, diagonally holding your opponent's wrist with your five fingers turned up.

Placing your other hand on the opponent's elbow, push his arm towards the ground.

Put your elbow close to the opponent's ear. The hand that pushed his elbow towards the ground should now slide underneath his arm, so as to grasp your own wrist, creating a strong lever.

Drag the locked hand back, and at the same time raise your elbow. Do not lift the hand from the ground, and keep your arm at as tight an angle as possible.

• INVERTED ARMLOCK

The opponent tries to push you, but unsuccessfully attempts a bridge and loses his balance. Put one of your hands on the ground as a support, and with the other hand grasp the wrist of the opponent's arm that is extended towards your chest.

2 Slide your leg under his face and start to lower your hips.

Twist your hips and torso, positioning yourself so as to face your opponent's legs. **3**

4

Gain firm hold of your opponent's wrist, pointing his thumb forward and pressing your hips in the same direction, finishing the inverted armlock.

• UNLOCKING FOR ARMLOCK

In choke position, you see the chance of executing an arm attack. Instead of placing your thumb inside the opponent's collar, put your hand on the ground as a support.

Pass your leg over your opponent's face. This may allow you to make a direct armlock or a defense, as seen in the picture. In this case, wrap your arm around your opponent's arm and grab his collar while moving back with your hand on the ground, on the same side of his head.

Start leaning your body weight diagonally backwards, pulling it against your opponent's arm.

If your opponent does not let go, put the foot that was over his stomach onto his biceps, pushing until you break open his grip, in order to facilitate the lock you are about to make.

Stretch his arm by lying back, finishing the armlock.

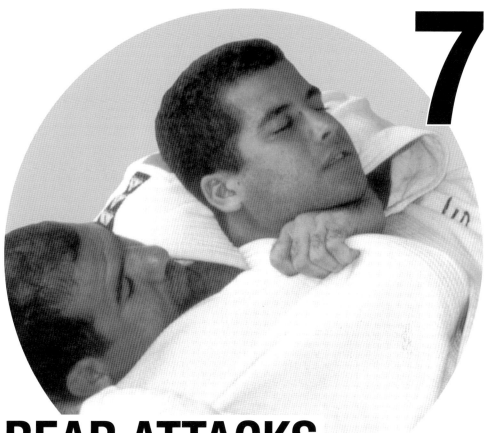

7

REAR ATTACKS

This is an extremely decisive position. To wisely carry on the fight at this point is almost to determine its result. For a successful rear attack, as in all other positions, you need to know different ways to escape in order to predict your opponent's moves and intercept them. There are many ways to win the fight through rear attacks, and placing your hand on the opponent's collar, over his shoulder, is part of all of them; this is precisely the first move you must try to make. Your next concern should be to keep your opponent in the position opposite that which offers him a chance to escape. You need only place your other hand correctly in order to create a second support, which will depend on the type of attack selected. Training for this technique must also be separate: exercise just the rear attack, if your opponent escapes; restart if you are able to finish it; restart again and keep going. You will feel a rapid progression and will be much more self-confident when attacking.

• REAR NAKED CHOKE

Start in mounted position.

Your opponent tries to turn. Let him do so, but keep your hands on the ground, with arms extended, in order to keep your balance. Raise your hips slightly, so as to allow him to turn.

Immediately after he turns, make two hooks with the feet inside your opponent's legs, putting your arm around his neck and grasping your own biceps.

Immediately place your other hand behind his head, with the palm turned towards you. Tighten the rear naked choke by pressing your elbows towards your chest and putting your hand on the back of his head, pressing it forward.

Observe the correct position of the hooks and see how it is also possible to apply the rear naked choke with your back on the ground.

• GUARD PASS TO BACK

The position begins at guard, where the main thing is never to let your opponent feel at ease. Prepare yourself by grabbing his wrist with both hands.

Put your foot on the ground on the same side of his pinned arm and move it diagonally, making room for a hip escape.

After moving your hips, put your arm around your opponent's back while retaining control of his other arm, preventing him from recovering his guard.

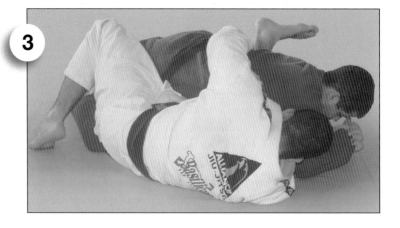

Put your head on the opponent's shoulder, grab his belt and continue to move your hips out from under him.

Place the second hook with your other leg while grabbing hold of your opponent's back.

The hand that you used to grab your opponent's belt must now go straight to his collar, while the other hand must grab the other lapel, thus achieving a choke.

• HOOK ATTACK OVER THE ARMS

Beginning
in all-fours
domination,
grab your
opponent's
wrist by slipping
your hand under
his armpit.

Place your leg over his arm, at the
same time putting your hand on his
collar.

Pull your
opponent
over the side,
make the hook
and gain a
better hold of
him, taking
advantage of
the fact that he
cannot defend
himself with his
hand, since it is
pinned by your
leg.

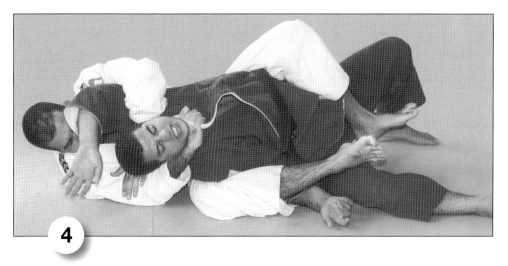

Extend the hand that was on the opponent's wrist on the back of his head, at the same time pulling his collar. You've got him!

• COLLAR CHOKE

Start in position with the hooks and the hands placed one over the shoulder and the other under your opponent's arm.

2 Pull on his lapel with the hand that was under his arm, so as to allow the other hand to get a grip deep into his collar with the thumb facing in. Place your head on the same side as the hand grasping the collar.

Pass the other hand, which is under the opponent's arm, to the other lapel and draw your hips towards the side of your head.

3

Pull both lapels, squeezing your opponent's neck. The hand that is under the arm holds the lapel as high as the opponent's chest, and should be driven down, while the other hand is pulled by placing your elbow on the ground and pressing your shoulder on the back of your opponent's head, always keeping your head close to his.

4

• ARMTRAP CHOKE

Start by positioning both hooks, with one of your hands placed over the shoulder and the other under your opponent's arm.

The hand that is under the opponent's arm is driven to the back of his head, with the palm facing you.

Escape with your hips and extend the arm on the back of your opponent's head, closing the elbow of the hand holding the collar. Draw your body away, extend both arms and tighten the choke.

• CLOCK CHOKE

With your
opponent on all
fours, hold his
wrist opposite
the side you are
on, sliding your
hand under his
arm.

Take note of the
position of your
knee between
your opponent's
elbow and
knee, so as to
keep him from
recovering his
guard.

Move in with
your other hand
in order to grasp
the opponent's
collar with your
thumb facing in,
always leaning
on his back with
all your weight,
so as to prevent
any reaction
from him.

Straighten your leg whose knee had been on the ground, extending it forward, while leaving your other leg in the same position, so that your two legs resemble the hands of a clock. Pull up the opponent's collar and lean over him with your head down, to keep him dominated until the end of the movement.

4

• CRUCIFIX

Your opponent is on all fours. Take control of his wrist on the side opposite you, placing your knee between his knee and his elbow.

1

Extend your leg, sliding it under his arm, so as to have his arm between your legs.

2

3 Put the hand that was on your opponent's wrist on the back of your head, crossing your legs and locking your opponent's arm between them.

Propping yourself up on the foot that was on the ground, throw yourself up and roll over your opponent's back.

4

5 Hold your opponent with his belly up and put your hand inside his collar, seizing it from behind his back and tightening the choke.

• SHOULDER LOCK

In an all-fours domination, put your knee between your opponent's elbow and knee.

Stretch your leg under his arm, and then bend it in order to pin his arm.

Release your opponent's wrist on the other side and execute a roll while facing outward. At this moment your opponent will begin to feel the lock.

4 Unless he wants to be finished then and there, your opponent will execute a somersault in order to relieve the pressure on his shoulder. Follow his movement and grab one of his legs in order to keep him down.

Gain control of the opponent's head, and with the other hand grab his leg. He will not be able to sit up, and you will have complete command over the situation.

5

6 Start to turn your body, facing your opponent and tightening the lock.

8

GUARD ATTACKS

Guard is one of the moments in Jiu-Jitsu where there is an excellent chance of finishing the combat. Countless armlocks and chokes are possible when this position is closed, that is, when your legs are interlocked behind your opponent's back. You must never let your opponent achieve a position in which he can stand up and extend his leg. This will allow for a great range of attack modes, in addition, of course, to the sweeps seen in Chapter 4. Open guard, in turn, is much more unpredictable because it offers many more options, making it much more dangerous: triangles and scapulas show up when you least expect them, armlocks occur just after a sweep defense, and so on. There is a saying: "Never rest in the middle of anybody's guard; it can be very dangerous." The combination of sweeps and attacks is almost infallible when done well!

• FRONT COLLAR CHOKE

With your opponent in guard, place
one of your hands on the back of his
collar with your palm facing up.

Slip the other hand in below the arm
that is already on the collar, also with
the palm facing up.

See in detail
how your hands
should be
placed.

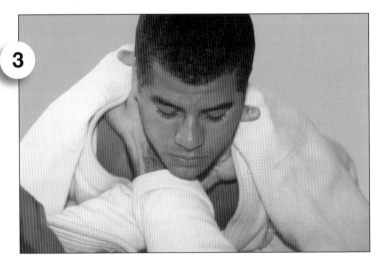

Draw your opponent towards you, using your legs to pull him in. Tighten the choke, touching his shoulder with your head and pressing him against your body to complete the choke.

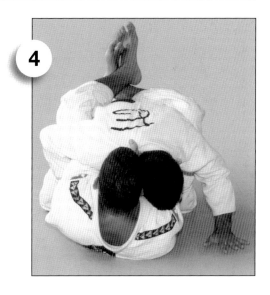

• ARMLOCK

Your opponent raises the leg opposite the arm that is extended against your chest.

Twist your arm around this leg, placing one foot on the opponent's groin and sliding your hips to the side of the arm being attacked, raising your other leg and placing it on his back.

3 Grab the opponent's wrist and move your leg past his face. Finish by placing both feet on the ground.

4

Finish the armlock, releasing the leg while holding your opponent's wrist with your two hands.

• STANDING ARMLOCK

Starting in closed guard, grab both of the opponent's arms and wait until he starts to stand up.

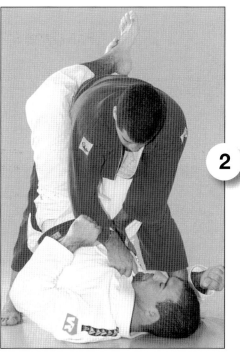

Grab your opponent's forward arm (the one on your chest) and put your other arm around his leg, enabling you to move your hips out and leave your back on the ground.

Move the foot on the same side as the arm you are about to attack to your opponent's hips, moving your other leg high up his back. Place your weight on your leg so as to keep your waist high and leave him no space to free his arm.

Move your leg in front of the opponent's face and place your weight on your feet, creating a lever and dominating his arm.

• KIMURA

1

The opponent places one hand on the ground inside your guard. Quickly grasp his wrist, with your five fingers turned up.

2

Open your guard, sitting diagonally while passing your other arm over the opponent's shoulder.

Twist your arm around the opponent's arm that you are holding, grasping your own wrist, always with your five fingers facing up, so that the opponent cannot extend his arm.

Move your hips out towards the side of your arm, forcing your opponent to put his face on the ground.

Place your leg over the opponent's back, to keep him from rolling out of your attack, pushing your pinned hand towards the back of his head and locking the Kimura.

5

• TECHNICAL CHOKE

Your opponent is in closed guard. Assume a sitting position and place your arm around his neck.

1

2

With your other hand over the opponent's shoulder, grasp your own wrist, making sure you feel that your arm is around his neck and not his chin.

3 See in detail how you should place your hands for the choke.

4

Lie back and extend your legs, raising your hips to increase pressure and achieve the choke, pressing the arm that is around your opponent's neck upwards with the help of the hand holding your wrist.

• HAND-IN-COLLAR CHOKE

Begin the attack when your opponent, who is on his knees, is in guard with both hands on the inside. Grab his sleeves with both hands.

Put one hand on his collar with the four fingers (all except the thumb) inside, bearing down with your legs on your opponent's arms.

3 Sit down and put your arm around your opponent's head, with your armpit over the back of his neck.

4

Move your hip towards the same side as your arm, leaning your body to the opposite side. Pull your opponent's collar by extending your arm, using your other arm to exert pressure on the back of his head, finishing the choke.

• CHOKE WITH WRAPPED-AROUND ARM

From guard, grab the opponent's collar at the same side as your attacking arm.

When your opponent tries to assume his desired stance, extend your arm under his, while pulling his collar down and breaking his posture. If you also use your legs, you will be able to pull him more effectively.

Put your arm around his, and grab the same lapel where your other hand had been. You should actually pass the lapel from one hand to the other.

3

4

Move your hips out to the same side as the pinned arm and put your other hand in, with the thumb inside the collar. Tighten the choke, moving your elbow towards your opponent's chest to keep him from using his other hand to resist.

• TRIANGLE

Your opponent tries to open your legs, placing one of his hands between them.

Place your foot on the opponent's groin on the same side as his arm, moving your other leg up and around his neck. Pull his arm diagonally.

Pull your foot with your hand, so that your calf is squarely on the back of his head, and then put your other leg over the foot you are pulling, so that your knee joint is directly over it.

Pull your opponent's head with both hands, pressing one of your knees towards the other and both towards your chest.

MOUNTED ESCAPES

We need to gain a better understanding of Jiu-Jitsu as a defensive fighting style. According to this principle, mounted escapes are of the utmost importance, since they deal with extricating oneself from difficult situations. Firstly, it is very important to keep cool. How to be cool with a 240-pound person mounted on top of you? The answer is that you have to know the technique in order to keep calm. If the technique is perfect (and I know it is!), why should you be frightened? If you understand this, you already have the advantage, and you will be able to consider how to achieve the best lever that fits a given situation. After that, it is a piece of cake, once the techniques fit together perfectly, as always, and your opponent will not be able to keep you dominated. This is an extremely important concept, which often defines the fight: if your opponent cannot win, he will fatally lose – there simply cannot be a draw!

• UPA (BRIDGE)

A mounted opponent moves one of his hands into your collar, grasping it in order to start an attack.

Grasp the opponent's wrist, keeping your elbow as close to the ground as possible. Grab your other arm by the shoulder, keeping your elbow closed.

Go into a bridge, leaving just your feet on the ground and bending your legs, and then roll over one of your shoulders. The hand that is on your opponent's shoulder helps you to pull him down, upsetting his balance even more.

Stand on your knees, pulling your opponent's wrist down in order to avoid any attempt he may make to choke you.

Finish your escape by assuming a guard position.

• ELBOW ESCAPE

Your opponent is mounted. Start shifting your body to the side, stretching one leg and stopping the opponent's thigh with the opposite hand.

Push the opponent's leg with your two hands and retract your leg that was stretched, escaping with your hips to the opposite side.

2

Lock the opponent's leg, as shown in the detailed view, and slide your hips to escape to the other side.

3

4

Stop your opponent's knee on the other side and retract your leg, which should be closed with the knee pointing up.

With your foot on the ground, move your hips **5** back towards the side of the leg that is still being held, pulling your arm and extending your body.

Extract your leg and lock the guard, **6** completing the successful movement.

• GUARD RECOVERY

The opponent has you in side control, with **1** one of his hands in front of your face and the other under your elbow, in a good dominating position.

Make a bridge by putting your outstretched arm in front of the opponent's face, so as to free your head, using your shoulder.

2

Slide your hips away, stopping the opponent's hips with an extended arm, thus creating a large space.

3

Move your leg out from under your opponent's body, turning your hips to the opposite side.

4

5 Complete the movement, extending your body, pulling the opponent's arm and locking your guard.

• REAR ESCAPE

The opponent has two hooks on your back. The first step is to protect your neck by placing your biceps against your ear, so that your opponent cannot slide his hand over your shoulder and into your collar or put his arm around your neck in order to attempt a rear naked choke.

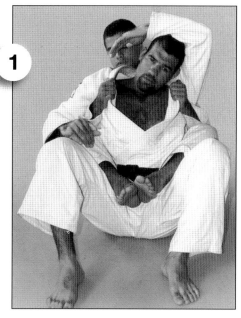

1

2 Make a bridge by raising your hips and placing your head on the ground, at the same side as the arm you used to defend yourself.

3 Still holding your hips high, use your hand to help undo the hook at the same side of your head, moving your hips out towards this side.

4 Stop your opponent's other knee with your hand, so that he cannot mount you, and slide your knee close to his chest. Keep moving your hips outwards.

5 Complete your escape, placing him on guard.

• LOCKED HEAD UPA (BRIDGE)

The opponent is mounted, hugging your head from over your face.

Grab his elbow with one of your hands, pulling it down, while supporting his hips with the other hand and keeping the elbow on the ground.

Start the Upa, making a bridge to the side of the dominated elbow, pushing the opponent's hips up with your hand.

Turn on your knees and fall into his guard, completing the escape.

4

• MOVE TO THE REAR FROM ALL FOURS

Begin the movement on all fours, with your head close to your opponent's legs. He is hugging your torso under your arms.

1

Put your arm around one of his, and extend the leg on the same side. Support yourself on the other arm, which you must place between your opponent's legs.

2

Put your head out, at the same time kicking your leg forward in a diagonal movement. Your head must be placed against your opponent's back.

3

4

Turn yourself around your extended leg in a V-shaped, compass-like movement, which takes you to the back of your opponent, putting you into an attack position.

• REVERSAL

Starting in side
control, note the
correct position
of your arms.
The knee on the
same side of
your opponent
must remain
always under
his waist. Your
other hand must
be placed under
the opponent's
armpit without
grabbing his
kimono, for this
would stop the
movement.

Always start
the movement
with a bridge,
creating the
necessary
space for you to
move your hips
out.

Move your hips out again and start
turning on your knees, with your
head inside and arm extended and
reaching for your opponent's leg.

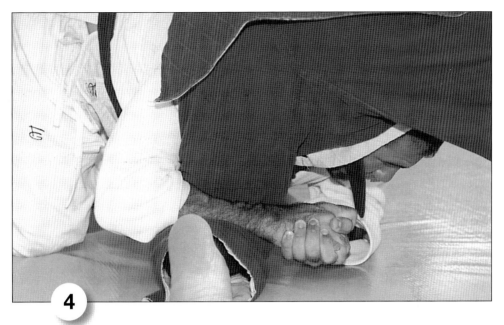

4

Kneel down and grab hold of your opponent's leg, drawing it towards your chest. Your head must remain drawn inward: you need it there to push the opponent's hips and force him to sit. This movement must be executed while drawing his leg towards your chest.

5

As a result, your opponent falls in a sitting position while you are over him with an almost-passed guard.

10

THROWS

The standing part, though not as decisive in Jiu-Jitsu—where it is worth just two points (as in Judo), is very important from the aspect of personal defense. It is becoming more and more a distinctive mark in Jiu-Jitsu competition, often allowing you to begin the fight in the upper position, which may be considered an advantage. Falls are clearly based on a lever principle, which the learner should master. This principle teaches a great deal about balance, achieving a good stance, which is essential for any fighter. Many tend to look down on this type of training, but I assure you it is as important as any other part of Jiu-Jitsu.

• O SOTO GARI

You and your opponent are standing
facing each other. If you are right-
handed, put your right hand on
his collar and your left hand on his
arm. If you are left-handed, do the
opposite.

Step forward with your left leg,
keeping it slightly bent and parallel
to your opponent's right leg. Pull him
slightly to your side, so as to transfer
his weight to his right leg.

3 With your toes turned down, thrust your right leg forward, passing it between your left leg and your opponent's right leg. Shift all your weight forward.

Move your right leg back, sweeping your opponent off his supporting leg. Remember to always keep your right foot over the ground.

4

5 At the same time, push down with the hand holding the opponent's collar, throwing him to the ground.

6 Finish the throw, holding your opponent's arm and standing upright.

• O GOSHI

Starting from the neutral position seen in the previous series, take one sidestep, at the same time wrapping your arm around the opponent's back and putting your head close to his chest.

1

2 Move your rear leg forward, so as to place your feet parallel to each other though inside the range of your opponent's separated feet. Bend your legs so that your hips are lower than his. This will make it easier for you to put him off balance.

Lower your head and straighten your legs, moving your hips slightly out. Then raise your head and lift your opponent off the ground. **3**

4 Turn your torso to complete the projection.

Grab your opponent's arm and keep your body straight. **5**

• KOSHI GURUMA

Starting from neutral position, put your arm around your opponent's neck. At the same time, take a diagonal step towards the same side as your arm.

Move your other leg back and slide your hips in, bending both legs, so that your opponent remains behind you and his base is more open than yours.

Raise your hips, extending your legs
and torso to achieve projection.

3

4

Finish by grabbing the opponent's
arm tightly and standing upright.

• IPPON SEOI NAGUE

Starting from neutral position, take a diagonal step, placing your arm under your opponent's. Do not grab anything: just trap his arm with the pressure of your biceps.

Put your other arm back and fit your hips against the opponent. Shift your weight forward, releasing it from your heels.

3 Stretch your leg, raising your hips and turning your torso to achieve the desired projection.

Finish with your body straight, grabbing your opponent's arm.

4

• DOUBLE LEG

Begin your move by taking a large step forward, without holding your opponent's kimono.

Move your rear foot close to the lead foot, reducing the distance.

Advance your foot again, moving your head sideways and out, closing on the opponent's hips and placing your hands behind his knee joints.

Project your
shoulders
forward and pull
your opponent's
legs towards
you, lifting him
off the ground.

4

5

Continue to
hold his legs,
but maintain
your balance at
the end of the
movement.

• DOUBLE LEG-TO-SHOULDER TAKEDOWN

Instead of reaching for your
opponent's kimono, prepare to
attack his legs, this being a good
attack choice at all times.

Take one step out and to the side of
your opponent's foot. At the same
time, place your head against his
hips on the opposite side of your
feet.

Do not try to lift him on your shoulder,
even though this is easier. First raise
the opponent's leg on the same side
as your head; this will shift all his
weight onto the leg that is still on the
ground.

Keeping your torso straight, drag his other leg in the same direction as the first. Always pull the opponent's legs toward the same side as your head.

4

5

Let the opponent down and fall directly upon him, giving him no time to go into guard after the fall.

• LEG GRAB AND HOOK

Start the position with the classic kimono grab.

Then start pushing your opponent back with the hand that is on his collar, taking one step forward with the foot on the same side. This will make your opponent step backward in order to regain control, leaving his front leg close to you and light enough for you to bend down to grab hold of it.

3 Stand up straight again, bringing the opponent's leg with you, lifting his foot off the ground. Take one step between his legs to reduce the distance.

Put in your hook behind his supporting leg and take it off the ground, at the same time pulling down on his collar in order to make him fall.

4

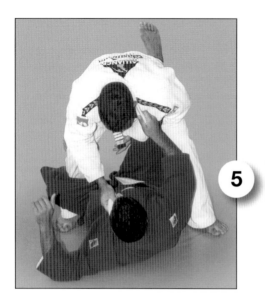

5 Throw the opponent down, while keeping yourself standing and in guard.

Fabio Duca Gurgel do Amaral

Eight-time World Champion Fabio Duca Gurgel do Amaral began practicing Jiu-Jitsu at the age of 13 and received his black belt at the age of 19. Along with his master, Romero Jacaré, he is the co-founder of the two-time World Champion Alliance Team with 40 academies around the world – from Venezuela to New York, from Finland to Germany. Gurgel continues to teach at his own academy in São Paulo and gives seminars throughout the world. He is president of the Professional League of Jiu-Jitsu.

"Fabio Gurgel to me is one of the best modern Jiu-Jitsu fighters of his time. He still competes and does very well at the masters division; he also represented Jiu-Jitsu against Wrestling in one of the best MMA matches of the 90s. He is my first black belt and a great friend. I am very grateful to God to have met him and have been able to touch his life."

Romero Jacaré